I249

PELT

Sarah Jackson was born in 1977, grew up in Berkshire and now lives in Nottingham. Her pamphlet *Milk* (Pighog, 2008) was shortlisted for the Michael Marks Award and her work appears in a number of magazines and anthologies, including *Voice Recognition: 21 Poets for the 21st Century* (Bloodaxe Books, 2009) and *The Best British Poetry 2011* (Salt Publishing, 2011). She was awarded Arts Council funding in 2009, has been shortlisted for the Arvon International Poetry Competition (2010), and was a runner up in the Edwin Morgan Poetry Competition (2011). Sarah completed a doctorate at the University of Sussex in 2009 and now lectures at Nottingham Trent University, where she runs the MA in Creative Writing. *Pelt* (Bloodaxe Books, 2012) is her first book-length collection.

SARAH JACKSON

PELT

BLOODAXE BOOKS

ISBN: 978 1 85224 931 1

First published 2012 by
Bloodaxe Books Ltd,
Highgreen,
Tarset,
Northumberland NE48 1RP.

www.bloodaxebooks.com
For further information about Bloodaxe titles
please visit our website or write to
the above address for a catalogue.

Supported by
**ARTS COUNCIL
ENGLAND**

Cover design: Neil Astley & Pamela Robertson-Pearce.

Printed in Great Britain by
Bell & Bain Limited, Glasgow, Scotland.

For Paul

And the men stepped out in colours up to their necks, pulling wet hides out after them so it appeared they had removed the skin from their own bodies. They had leapt into different colours as if into different countries.

MICHAEL ONDAATJE
In the Skin of a Lion

ACKNOWLEDGEMENTS

Acknowledgements are due to the editors of the following publications in which some of the poems – or variations of them – first appeared: *1110, The Arvon International Poetry Competition Anthology 2010, The Echo Room, Envoi, The Frogmore Papers, Interpreter's House, Irish Pages, Magma, New Walk, The New Writer, The North, Other Poetry, Poetry South, The Rialto* and *Staple*.

'Remains' was awarded a runner up prize in the Edwin Morgan Poetry Competition 2011. 'Ten O'Clock Horses' was commended in the same competition. 'Into the Horse' was shortlisted for the Arvon International Poetry Competition 2010. Some of these poems first appeared in the pamphlet *Milk* (Pighog, 2008), which was shortlisted for the Michael Marks Award 2009.

I am grateful to the Arts and Humanities Research Council, the Arts Council, and Cove Park for their support. I would also like to thank all the family, friends, and colleagues who have inspired and encouraged me during the writing of this book, in particular to Polly Clark, Brendan Cleary, Abi Curtis, Jane McKie, Miles Mitchard, Karen Schaller, Mahendra Solanki, Bethan Stevens and Gregory Woods.

CONTENTS

III *Dreamed some rain so I could sleep*

IV *Hear me out*

I

If I chance to talk a little wild, forgive me

WILLIAM SHAKESPEARE
King Henry VIII

Vanishing Twin

For years, I've hid
in a cracked hotel
tipping the moors.

I sleep days, among piles
and piles of laundry;
nights, I steal dreams,

wrap them up
in soft white towels,
longing for you,

my duck egg girl,
my vanishing twin.
Do you remember me?

I still feel the ache
of your lidless space,
your imprint on my skin.

The Red Telephone

(after Gary Young)

The boy stands at the bottom of the stairs clutching an apricot in his right hand so tightly that the juice runs down between his fingers. In his left hand he holds a toy telephone. It is red plastic with a curly white cord. It rings when you pull it along the ground by its string.

The boy pretends to telephone his mother who is upstairs in the bathroom, changing her tights because she has a ladder in her heel. *Fall down*, he whispers. *Fall down*. And I swear to you, when her kneecaps crack the bathroom tiles, the small red telephone rings.

Ten O'Clock Horses

At night, our village is packed
in rows like fish at the market,
flat on our backs. In the attic
I am scaled with moonlight,

waiting for the horses to ride
over the black earth. They snort
outside the room where I go
to love my secrets in the absolute dark,

where spiders squat in solitude,
cursing at the two moons
under my nightdress
as I open my mouth,

breathe hard and look up
between the slats in the roof
at the clouds kissing the stars.
Hurry child, my mother says.

The ten o'clock horses are coming.
She is knitting socks without heels.
At ten, Father blows out the lamp,
my secrets still steaming.

Thirty of the king's best horses,
he told me, but he won't talk
of his own mysteries, even when I ask.
Later, when he is hard at his hush-hush,

I close my eyes and watch
the horses slip from his tongue,
land with a click on the cobbles,
their hooves clinking like coins

in his pocket, or teeth falling out.
First he snuffs the lamp.
Then he snuffs my mother.
She lands softly, like teeth.

Her needles clatter like thirty tiny horses
galloping over tiny cobbles,
like the sound of my father's money
falling from her mouth.

Two Mothers

(after Paula Rego)

One just crawled into my cot,
laid her head in my lap.
I'm tired, she said.
I sweep away the hair
that cracks her cheek.
Her old eyes close.
I smile, hold onto her head,
gather her to me
as dark walks past the window.

I have another mother below
who is cleaning walls, singing,
her tight, white hips spinning,
while this one sleeps.

Too big for my bed
she's a coal sack leaking milk,
skirts mashed between slumped legs,
hands huge, wider than my face.
Her arm falls out of the cot,
too fat to fold back. She won't wake
and though toothless, I bite her.
I don't mean to make her cry.

There's not room for us both
and cold, hairless, hungry,
I slip through the bars easily.
Though I have two mothers
neither hears me climb in
with the boneless dolls,
close the toy-box lid.

What Daddy Built

That night the dogs cried again and woke you.
Wanting to be still-small you climbed inside the doll's house
that Daddy built. Sunk below your bed line, it waited, floored.

In the darkness your bed was a long, hard road
and you belly-crawled on all fours as if you were still a baby.
Hem rucked around your gut, you were naked under a pale purple nightie,

the owl at the window watching you creep.
Your big-girl body was a white worm, big-girl skin rubbing nylon,
static cracking up the dark with tiny forks of yellow

like yellow-boned fingers with long yellow nails
and where your big-girl bed fell away you dropped to the floor.
The dogs cried again and blind, you reached out, found the house

that Daddy built. You stroked its door, finger-felt its floor,
placed your cheek on glossy gables. You ran your tongue-tip
all up the walls, bit down, the wood splinters sweet, cool.

You licked the shiny red roof and it was so slick it slid nearly
deep inside you. Truly, you could eat this doll's house that Daddy built
or it could eat you. And then you unhooked the door, reached inside

to touch the doll people, the length of your arm
folding right into its hot, red belly. Finally you slept,
your head in the kitchen window, a doll in your teeth.

Into the Horse

(for Anna)

Sister, I dreamed we were birds again
and mother fed us worms, our beaks
wide open like Japanese fans.

Sister, I dreamed I was swallowed
into the horse again and you were there
to light my candle and take my hand.

Sister, I dreamed it rained again
and we danced barefoot beside the chateau
while father fetched us honey.

Sister, I dreamed I was a stray again.
You stole me into in your blue room,
bandaged my greasy paw with your ribbon.

Sister, I dreamed we were dolls again,
that grandfather painted eyelashes
on our cheeks, and we slept in a glass cot.

Sister, I dreamed we wore nylon again,
sharing electric theatres in the dark,
knowing nothing of our sons, of their death.

Sister, I dreamed we were close again,
that we poured into each other like cold milk
from the red breakfast jug.

Sister, I dreamed we shared a terror again.
I dreamed we shared a tongue.
I dreamed we shared a skin.

Sister, I dreamed we fed the chickens again.
I was not afraid of their eyes
and you let me carry the eggs.

Crabbing

Maybe she thinks I'm peeing
but I'm not. I'm crouched
behind a clutch of rock pools
with a hermit crab, while
she's griddled on a towel,
not seeing my best red suit
bum-dipping the water,
which is warm, green,
and sliding over the rocks
like the white of an egg.

There's my name again –
so large and pink inside her mouth,
though wetter at the edges
than when she calls me
in changing rooms – licked up
by the wind, quailing across
the blue-grey stretch. I duck
down lower, pull the crab
out of the brown sea-snail shell
by ten bunched-up legs

until he slides out with only a hint
of suck. Then I hold him up
to the sun, squint at the eyes
dropping from his face
like two pinpricks of blood,
the long, soft belly
and that strange nub,
which starts just below his heart
and opens out at the last pair
of purple walking legs.

Night Fishing

My father sails a boat curved like a cradle,
paints eyes on the bow to ward off evil.
He mends sails with Grandma's wedding dress.
The mast is polished oak: tall, dead-straight –
the barrel of a shotgun. Splitting
the estuary into open waters, the hull
glistens with sea-bream, beautiful fat cod.

I sleep right here in the brown cardboard box
stowed beneath his tiller. I am small, snug, the tip
and roll of waves running through my marrow.
Every night, I wait for my father to tidy his nets,
part his legs and look down at me lying upturned
like a little trout, my belly slick with sea salt.
Hello shrimp, he says, then tells me about my mother:

She had a thin smile like the fold of a fish-fin,
a saltiness that gathered between her back-teeth
and sometimes, during long clear nights,
fishermen still see the length of her arms,
her gleaming face, as she offers herself to the ocean –
her back strapped to a polished oak mast,
her arms fastened to sails of white lace.

Old Fatty Knees

She's easy to sail – lively enough in light air, tacking
and jibing smoothly with virtually no leeway – and most
importantly, safe even in rough weather.

FATTY KNEES BOAT COMPANY

So Archie took me on board
his Fatty Knees, taught me
how to raise her mainsail,
the names of all her ropes.

Crouching in the hull
was like being born, the boat
moist and fat-bottomed
but tapered to a T where she nosed

the dark water between Moulsford
and Streatley lock, my palms
gripping her sides as he showed me
how to tack, jibe

and I asked again to be taken home.
Every Sunday for months
I dreaded the cold, the damp,
yet never knew why

until I turned into the wind,
watched the boom crack the back
of his head and the way his hand
reached out for his own face.

19

Wingspan

When it rains your parents call you inside
for dinner. You are curled with the wet

greyhound beside the pond. The fish
seem to be multiplying, like shadows.

＊

In the winter, the pond freezes over.
A heron lands on the ice, his foot

tangling in fishing wire. You watch
as your parents, huge in their winter coats,

flap outside with secateurs.
The heron's wings are as wide

as their car. And the noise:
it is your mother beating the carpet.

The heron looks at you and begs.
There is a readjusting of knowledge.

＊

You leave in the spring.
Your parents wave with their whole arms

the way adults do to children,
the way the heron rose up above you.

Like a Smile

Mother in a yellow
sweater turns blue
then black beneath
the climbing frame
weaver ants pouring
out of her nose
but I don't

breaking a beer bottle
on the toilet bowl
I finger the lovely slab
of slippery green
test the sharp lilt
on the inside
of a pink and white

wearing my skin
like a smile I visit
mother in her yellow
sweater – come here
she says – I haven't
given you a proper
hello yet

Leftovers

The second Saturday of every month
they remind me how to work the remote,
point out the rocket salad with walnut and blue cheese,
kindly suggesting I don't touch
the thermostat or the baby.
Then they go to friends' for dinner
or to that nice little Thai place on the corner
of Bridge Street, just the two of them.

Watching *Casualty* on widescreen
I thumb through last year's holiday snaps
left out under the solicitor's letter.
I sidestep the salad but sip Sauvignon Blanc
from an open bottle,
eat Cheerios out of the packet,
fat fingers greasy with spit.
At a quarter to, I check the baby
is breathing.
Watching him feels like spying
and I sit on stripped pine floors
pretending it's all mine.

They rattle the keys as a warning.
Warmed by wine she offers me a drink,
insists I stay.
We can have a proper chat over breakfast, she says.
Yes, she says, as she always does, do stay.
In the spare room, I undress, wait,
listen for the sounds of them breathing.

Night hums softly
and by dawn my legs are wound around
the white silk of her wedding gown.

Touch Papers

It is white when I wake
so I wear my old navy dufflecoat,
finding them in my pocket
tucked inside a brown envelope.

Here she is. Squatting,
she is the callus
on her size seven heel,
fingers tinsel-chipped

from schoolboard chalk,
driftwood nails, thumb
a pumicestone mouse
smiling my cheek.

Here he is. Flat out,
he is the lip of his ear,
swan soft, dust flecked,
the sound of a dog pawing.

He has grey whiskers that beat
like hair on coral
and his eyelid when he blinks
is deep, pooling, purple.

I hold them inside my pocket,
fondle skin letters
climbing the library steps.
They barely make a sound,

a rustle, a peep, as I slip
them between the pages
of a dictionary, under
Mother, Father.

Revolution

we revolt at night unzipping our red silk skins
turning the pearly ridges of our backs on the moon
white knuckles hovering in a hall of black tulips
there are hoards of us & I'm in charge of the bones

we slither on our limp bellies down to the crocus fields
the touch of our bald bodies making the grass roots sing
if they see us coming they'll beat us with feathers again
we revolt at night unzipping our red silk skins

the old birds live in the flowers with rotten wings
but shorter than grass we quiver on through
nosing in nests tucked inside the damp dark soil
turning the pearly ridges of our backs on the moon

I haven't eaten for years & I am starving hungry
oh listen I tell you I haven't eaten for years
so I strangle the blackbird & dig out its bones
white knuckles hovering in a hall of black tulips

there is a cracked-up moon swimming in here
and a wing bone reaches out of the night to gag me
it is quite sharp & could easily slit my slack-skin throat
only there are hoards of us & I'm in charge of the bones

II

I have my heart on my fist
Like a blind falcon.

ANNE HÉBERT
'The Tomb of the Kings'

Friday 12.03

You and I will meet
unexpectedly outside
the glass library
on Jubilee Street
and we will smile
shyly as the clock
inches forward to 04,
then we will blink
and feel it catch
in our lashes.

Around us the toddler,
the builder, the tramp
will feel it too:
these small soft beads
of white settle
on our hair, our cheeks,
and in that second
we will look up
only it won't be snow,
nor dust, nor light

but something else
entirely: something
our mothers never
taught us, a feeling
we can neither know
nor name, a deep settling
that will frighten us
yet make us smile
at each other
all the same.

The Instant of My Death

The bus was crammed and the fat man rubbed against my leg like
     a damp cat
while you read *The Jataka Tales* three rows from the back

and we all stumbled on, wheels and hours grinding, tripping
as Spiti rose up around us, sky propped open by its peaks.

I traced the rockline on the window with my finger,
counted cows and gompas, felt my eyes glaze over

until we reached Gramphoo. There, where the road divided
I saw a thin boy in red flannel squat between two dhabas;

a black-eyed bean, slipped in between two crags, he was so small
that I almost missed him, until he turned, gap-toothed, and shot me

with a toy gun. A piece of me stopped then, though the bus moved on
and the fat man beside me cracked open an apple with his thumb.

Momos and Tea

Afterwards, breaking through the skin of a 30-watt beam,
we walked out and into the middle depths of night

and stumbling across a ditch or a creek or a child,
we ducked into the Whispering Willow Café at the edge of Old Kaza

where a group of bug-eyed men and three Israeli tourists
talked in low voices, a dim light humming then blinking out.

When the waiter lit the candle, he glowed up good and bright,
his face utterly smooth, his eyes creaking a little as they met mine,

and glancing up I saw that I was alone inside a dream box
with padded walls and ceiling like the mattress of our bed.

The waiter was very sorry: there was nothing he could give us
except momos and tea. We ate and drank quickly,

listening to the small sounds of our sipping, before stripping
back the dusty notes, peeling ourselves apart

and slipping back into the darkness that hung there between us,
stumbling on and on through the night.

Sacred Cow

Wrapped inside a hawthorn nest on the bottom lip
of a mountain you find me waiting and shaking

and still holding my apple as I look up,
see the bruised peak rip open clouds and spill

the monsoon rains all over again. Chuckling at my crown
of thorns, rain slopping down my face, you clack with the toads

as you untangle me. Your lips are older than the earth,
your hand is worn raw as you take me

over rocks, sloshing in flooded gullies and tilting
through trees to a cowshed that smells hot and wet.

You lead me inside, where it is still, except for the cow's tail swaying
and your dark black braid swinging and the steam rising up

and up, as I try to memorise the shape of my left foot
on a rock slab, the white of my apple core in the mud,

which bubbles and breathes as I crouch beside you
and your black-eyed honey-skinned beast. She blinks and shivers

when you touch her. Squatting, you lay your flat palms
on her stretched stomach, rest your cheek on her soft flank,

murmur into her velvet skin. And I think you will drink her then,
as the rain drinks up all sound, and you and I and the cow, we melt

into the darkness until we are utterly silent
except for our swallowing.

Zooid

We ambled from Café des Fleurs
where the slow dog lived
and found ourselves at the beach
which was breathing with bodies
in floral suits. I had to close my eyes
against the giddiness of it
but when I looked up
I saw a Portuguese Man o' War
in the sky – an air bladder floating
over the hoards as we flopped about
drunk as seals. I watched back,
noting the way it moved –
filmy and tinged with mauve
like my grandfather's cataracts.

Monte Alcudina

The wind tears the tent from our fists as we pin it down
with rocks and boots and horses, who hang around, noses
dipping as if drilling us for oil. We speak mostly in silence,
words whipped from our mouths. It is half four and hot,
yet there is nothing to do but climb inside and fasten the
doors. Even then, the wind batters our backbones like pulses
in a jar, and when you release the zip for a breath in the
swelling heat I see a horse flung off the mountain as if it is
made of tin.

In the morning, everything is still, as though waiting. We
pretend this does not make us more afraid. We shake the
dust off everything, turn ourselves inside out and flap about
like two old wives doing the linen. We do not speak of the
clouds.

Cow Uprising

We lumber our colossal packs over a bed frame,
springs dripping with rust; climb, hanging passing thoughts
on the branches of Laricio pines, dipping in and out
of pockets of sun, heading south to Col de Saltu.
Before we even reach the gap, we almost pitch in to her:
a body reduced to half a head, a skin of broken boots.
Flies pour through the napkin ring of her trunk and I know
she would have fallen somewhere else if she could.
We march on until my feet throb and I sink like a dead cow
in the path of walkers. My husband's hands urge blood
back into my joints. He tells me that during the uprising
the villagers set their own cattle alight. I wake to find
he has vanished and the only sound is a cow crying:
her low song winds its tongue around the slopes.

Light Over Ratcliffe

The turnip field is water-logged. We sink
the further we get from the track. Eye-whites

of root vegetables lift from the black loam
and I dunk the green tops in their graves,

more wet than mud, the whole field swallowing
and I'm glad. I want the earth to take me in.

It'll be dark soon enough. The horses are napping.
The furrows lead us over a grass-topped bridge

and back onto a railway track that rips open
the gut of the field. Tripping the sleepers

we follow it home, hearing the haunt
of a train shunt the space between us.

Passing a copse that criss-crosses through dusk
we near the farm with the dogs. He twists at last

to look at me, but his eyes slip over the top
of my head, and his smile carefully unfastens.

He turns me as in bed. A vast white glare
breathes over the towers, a luminous cloud

lifting and smelting our faces, and in the instant
it takes to reach him, I am already blind.

Howling

You always say I should move –
a caravan on a cliff is no place for anyone,
least of all someone like me.

I like it here: the wind
storming bicycles over Beachy Head,
small dogs lurching into trees.

Perched on the nape of the Seventh Sister,
my teeth are dry; licking them
reminds me of the day we first met –

you picking me up like driftwood,
your eyes so kind
I thought I'd die of it.

Bringing me back you filled
my plastic cup with Dalwhinnie
because my throat was cracked

and I couldn't say why.
Now every Sunday you're back,
curbing my axle, tweaking my nose weight,

begging me to move.
I'd never leave this wind.
Tonight, we listen to the gale

howling the cliff, my teacups
knocking against Styrofoam walls,
tap-tapping us to sleep.

My encyclopaedia slumps sideways
above my foldaway bed
and our teabags quiver like voles.

Night Parliament

Every night, I devote myself to owls.
I know they have forward facing eyes and ears.

I know they have hairs on their beaks
for feeling and teeth on their feathers

for reducing noise. Every morning
I wake to discover how small

our bed has become under the sky,
how it is piled with clothes and children

who lift themselves only to squat
on the stairs and mewl for scraps of meat.

Stirring porridge, my eyes are yoked
in their sockets and I long to swallow

my husband whole. My mouth is a beak.
Speaking is for covering up my thoughts

with sounds. In rain I take to hiding in barns
and in wind I am blown across fields.

Doubles

Remember that we spoke of all this on those quick grey afternoons
watching for our doubles in the broken windows of the warehouse

across the road, breathing in the sweet brown blood of apples wrapped
in newspaper and stored in the eaves with my father's photos of Egypt.

One afternoon we watched a girl with bones too big for her face
hunt for pennies. Two Indians held hands in the rain. I licked you then

and told you of those long hot journeys across France. Our parents –
younger than we are now – had no idea how tonight would begin.

Remember that we spoke of all this and tossed coins to make decisions.
Back then we slept in a simple bed, made simple shapes with our bodies.

I told you I was wearing my dreaming boots and you smiled and made
simple sounds with your teeth. In the night, we threw pennies into the road.

III

Dreamed some rain so I could sleep.

LI-YOUNG LEE
'My Clothes Lie Folded for the Journey'

Carrying My Bones

I pitch on deck, where two men in Gortex talk about fixing
bicycles and one changes his T-shirt in the black wind.

We're heading to Kilcreggan tonight, only I think about
not going, about entering the water face-first instead.

You're waiting slantwise on the pier as I stumble,
dog-tired across the bridge. It's like walking over a body.

I can't keep my balance and there are oceans in my head.
You offer to take my bag but I'm carrying my own bones

in this suitcase of skin. I'm here to lock myself away
in water, although my mouth is a smile nailed in place.

You drive me to a cottage hung on the hill,
enough kindness to make my blisters weep,

but when you leave I grip the taps, twist them like wrists,
feel the cold rush of my house fill to its brim.

The sheep watch at the window as my face pushes the glass,
all bloated cheeks. Bleats leak from their stitched-up lips

as I double-knot my hair to the leg of the bed
and catch fish in my ribs.

Silent Running

In the half hour before she rises
a submariner cannot drop a comb
for fear of echo. Down there

it all depends on silent running.
In the pitching dark,
nothing but the crying of fish,

throat-murmurs of boats.
They're as deep as can be,
holding a steady trim,

seeing only the blood
in their brains. Air is short,
the darkness wide,

and they cannot blink too fast
for the sound of their eyelids
shudders the North Sea charts.

Miles and miles of night,
pegging for jabber or clack
of passing trawlers.

They might be moles
but the silence gives them back
their eyes, the twitch of their hearts,

and when the sky has bled
all scratch of light,
a man surfaces, opens the hatch,

enters the lean-to of black
and listens to the ocean
filling up.

Traces

You've not seen this before:
the sky flexing, breathing,
sucking in the sea like a tongue,

so you walk over the stones,
down and then out over the great flat
to where the old black pier crumbles

and you stand beneath the red sky
while the gulls pick for worms.
There are dozens of them, and just you

watching their claws make Ws in silt,
until you walk away slowly, frightened
by the letters your prints leave in sand.

Beachcombing

Today, I find a baby
rising out of the water

in her blue-bagged plastic,
tangled in spray cans,

dead man's fingers,
tarpaulin. Slung ashore

by conger eels,
she's barnacled to a rock,

cradled in fishing hooks
& pieces of polished glass

that reflect the hawks
of my eyes. She's

always looking at me,
even when I turn my back.

The curlews can't bear it.
Oil slicked across her skull

& skin white as teeth,
she never flinches at rain.

I carry her up the hill
under my shirt,

feel the tug & pluck
of our bodies.

We lie in my bed
sucking on toes & fingers,

gasping at the watery
secrets of daughters.

The Way Through Walls

I spend the winter watching birds
peck crusts from the snow. This island
is full of bracken and buzzards.

There are no newspapers here.
The shopkeeper says there's no need.
Lines of sadness fall from his mouth.

I put all my books in the bath,
afraid the ivy has found a way in
through the walls, and when

I discover a thrush in the fireplace,
her feathers fleeced in ash,
I dream of starlings unhooking

their nests from the trees,
carrying them in their beaks
across the murmuring ocean.

November

I'm not entirely alone. The matron
sails back and forth through the fog
like a warship. I squint,
try to read the name on her file.

Other than that, nothing happens
except rain, which hangs from the trees
as an experiment. Every night
at eight, someone turns out the light

and they sharpen their pencils.
I heard somebody calling once
and I don't know, perhaps a dog,
barking. It sounded far off.

Some days, I plan to break out,
but they say the walls are solid
bone reinforced with white paper.
Besides, I've seen their binoculars.

Instead, I curl up like a nut.
Yesterday, I found if I drop things
they make a noise but never break.
Later, I'll drop myself from the ceiling.

Visitor

You won't hear her.
She moves in time with the wind,
treads when the branches of the oak
snarl against the window,
skinning the chipped green frame.

You won't mind her.
She carries her hands like gloves,
her woollen socks are chickweed
bunched about her ankles, and you're sure
she's never slept in her bed.

You might not even know she's here
except for the smell of salt,
the tarn by the table,
her dripping hem, and the spills
of her steps to the door.

You won't notice her leave,
only the pattern of her breath
frosting the window in the shape
of the loch, and the damp
of her bones caught in the air.

Clam

The beach at night is my body.
You taught me this
and how goose barnacles
will slit your wrists
if you're not careful.

Tonight I'm fused with clams.
They stick upright like my sister's
fingernails or bunches of car keys
and when I try to run away from myself
they slice the soles of my bare blue feet.

I've never seen so much water:
it sluices through my bones
like your sperm, your spit,
cold crawling up inside me,
coming home in my chest.

You taught me about molluscs too,
how they have tongues for feet
and kill dog whelks
by tethering them to rock
until they starve to death.

You always find me.
Dragging me out of the sea again,
the water pours out of me again,
your boots snapping the clams
like children clapping.

Footing

The earth is soft
and I am sinking.
Beneath the mountain

the Chinese keep
engineered diseases
and black tanks.

Days pass without sign.
It is silent except
for water, aeroplanes.

Hours I do not sleep,
watch the submarines
slip by down there

like titanium eels.
Some days I smell
anthrax in the trees.

IV

Hear me out: that which you call death
I remember.

LOUISE GLÜCK
'The Wild Iris'

Operation Dark Harvest

behold, the hand of the Lord is upon thy cattle which is in the field,
upon the horses, upon the asses, upon the camels, upon the oxen, and
upon the sheep: there shall be a very grievous murrain

an animal losing the power of its back legs
a boil that turns black
a carcass washed up in the bay
a compulsory purchase
a devil with all the best weapons
an envelope packed with compensation
a flotilla of eighty sheep
a galvanised bucket of soil
a girl watching across the ocean with her windows taped shut
a high wall
an incinerator of bones
an island soaked in formaldehyde
the Junior Minister of Defence
Keep Out signs
a live one
a man cradling a beast
non-clotting blood
an occasional feeling of pressure in the chest
an open secret
periodic checks
a promise: I will carry you in both arms
quarantine
running the other way
a sheep in a boat
a sheep in a wooden coffin with a hole for its head
a small bomb and a puff of smoke
a soldier with his arms outstretched
a strange smell
and three days later they're back to count the dead
topsoil in sealed containers
two hundred and eighty pounds of contaminated soil, awaiting
        distribution

ultimately, hypovolemic and septic shock
a vicar reciting the plague of pestilence
Vollum 14578

and it became a boil breaking forth with blains upon man, and upon beast

The Farm

It starts when the children go blackberrying,
return with mouths smeared with milk.

It snows more. The scientists move us
into the old slaughterhouse at the farm.

They count us slowly, with clickers.
We're arranged in rows. Click. Click.

When they shuffle out with plastic bags
over their shoes, the dust plumes

behind their vans like flour. Later,
we find they've cut the telegraph wires.

The sun is white, our shit is white.
My children open their mouths to yawn

and their tongues are white. Look,
I tell my husband. Soon, they make us

count ourselves. Another baby is born
bloodless, breathless. We daren't scream.

The nights are white. We can no longer
see the stars. I can't hear the birds.

Host

(Deserted Hotel, Shabla, Bulgaria)

The wind here is devastating.

Hoarding sand on the sills
of a hotel beaten back by shrieks

it brings with it
a certain smell, a certain ring.

Nobody is here.

There is no waiter.
Nobody dances, nobody sleeps.

Just you and me
lying in the dust of the restaurant
holding ourselves –

and out there
the ocean rising and falling

rising and falling
like the skin over our ribs.

My Father's House

Inside, everything is wicker,
dead chrysanthemums in the hall.

His wife takes my waterproof mac,
offers saccharine with my tea.

The knobs on the kitchen cupboards
are frosted. On the work-top,

a Kenwood soda-stream.
She makes scrambled eggs for lunch –

it was his favourite, she tells me
as if I never knew him at all.

'Do you want to look at his papers,
root through his clothes?'

Instead, I ask about the garden.
It's just a patio, she says, and I remember

rolls of chicken-wire, spades.
I'm offered the spare room

but can't sleep. I listen for her step
on the stairs; hours later, his.

Mapledurham Lock

My mother watches canoes
and an ice cream drips down her wrist
while I look for myself in the river
finding I have aged
although my shadow is much the same.

Do you know, she says,
years back, it flooded and a boy drowned.

We watch for a flash of fins along the salmon ladder
and I have this feeling my arms are getting longer.

She mops herself with a green spotted hanky,
thoughts pouring down and pooling
in the creases of her skin.

Trailing back we talk openly of barren fields,
of hope and grief,
until a hesitation lodges between us like a tooth.

Everything is settled now, she says. She reaches
for my hand.

There will always be rain.

The Most Quiet

(after John Taggart)

a girl is late for the French class
a girl is late

and the young man leads his new wife under the temple
into the dust under the temple

a girl is late and boys kick a football in the dust
under the temple in the most quiet

a girl is late and the young man leads his new wife
into the French class into the most quiet French class

and boys kick a football in the dust
and cats curl around their ankles under the temple

in the most quiet
in the French class

a girl is late a girl is most quiet
and the cats' tails are scythes and the boys are dust

a girl is late for the French class and the teacher hides
and the young man kicks the dust under the temple

a young man leads his new wife into the French class
and the teacher kicks the dust

a young man leads his new wife under the temple
and the boys are most quiet

and the cats are scythes
and the girl bleeds softly into the dust

a girl bleeds
a girl is most quiet

a girl is late for the French class
the young man leads his new wife into the dust

Cave of Ears

Dripping with green
the moss ribs the rock walls
with jealous filaments.

On days like these,
when I lack moral fibre,
the best place for me

is the hole behind the waterfall.
Here, I hunker down,
recite auxiliary verbs

in a cave lobed with spores,
like a mouth filled with a thousand
ears, none of them listening.

I Have Not Yet Discovered

It was blood, it was
what you shed, Lord.

It shined.

                PAUL CELAN, 'Tenebrae'

This morning, I went to bathe
and found the basin filled with blood, Father.

It shined.

In it I saw the round hole of my mouth.
I have a slow, dumb smile.

These days, I have no eyes.
The two men stood at the window and watched.

The men watched me, so I cupped my hands
and ladled the shining blood to my face.

I washed in the blood
and the two men watched.

I do not know whose blood it is.
I have not yet discovered.

I washed my hands, my face, and my body,
especially my breasts. I washed out all my crying.

Listen: the morning bells were ringing, and I filled
the jug with blood, and poured it over my hair.

I combed my long, brown hair. I had grown it
for my wedding. So now, if I bend right back

it almost touches my heels. The men
leaned closer. I almost saw them, Father.

Truly, they shined.

I closed the shutters
and dressed as slowly as I dared.

Vocal Chords

I breakfast at the side of the house
where an old Breton plaque rusts

in the gravel beneath the window,
and there, flies worship the sparrow,

which lies, head bent right back
with its beak snapped clean off

like the lid of the margarine tub.
I bend down, lift the beak

between my finger and thumb,
look into the hollow of its throat

to see its vocal chords nestling
like a peach stone, wondering

where music comes from,
and where my voice has gone.

Cinder

Who would still dare run the risk of a poem of the cinder?
JACQUES DERRIDA

After the fire, the mountain is scorched.
You can barely look at it, only glassed in the eye
of the raven circling overhead. Then a fine grey ash
settles on the maquis and a single nuthatch pecks
for spiders in the cinders. You do not know how you got here,
cannot understand the strange geometry of two charred trees
laddering the blue. You press your ears to the earth,
listen for the cinder quarks, hear the klang, the hum.
In Cervione, they tied a camera to the bell tower
to swivel and picture the raging. Fire spreads like a heart.
Even the dictionaries are burning and now this grey dust,
this poem, this inaudible call. You sense its heat.
You hear it hissing. Take it in your mouth. Feel
the burning within language, the way it crumbles, falls.

Turn Out the Light

And the heron-man
will be watching you sleep.
His long fingers will twist
your neck, peel your scalp
with his silver butter knife.
Slowly, he will draw out your dream
and crack it open on the side
of his blue china teacup.

Bonjour Julia, he will say,
greetings to your bonnet of bees.
Listen carefully, do what I say:
you must unbind your fingers,
place your cheek on my paper.
When you dream you will write,
and you will wake
wanting to uproot trees.

Kola Superdeep

You say I should go down farther still, but I am already very deep down.
FRANZ KAFKA

After twenty-four years
of drilling, the borehole sits
like a navel in the dust.
A nudge, and it could swallow
a city, draw it hurtling in.

And to think you do not notice
the entrance, but suddenly find
you are inside, descending,
leaving traces of skin on granite
as you reach for each hold.

You have removed your shoes.
Yet not only your shoes.
You have left your telephone
on a ledge, can no longer hear
it ring. Now shed your nakedness

and everything that hides
beneath that. When the hole
narrows into a tunnel,
peel down by touch
as if you are unravelling.

I feel I should warn you:
there is no way out of this.
You will never arrive
and you are already far,
far away from home.

Remains

… après ma mort, il ne restera plus rien

JACQUES DERRIDA

1

Today, I find I can see through my eyelids.
You are curled over yourself as if reading

but there is no book. I wait, counting the dogwood
on the curtain, listening for the telephone.

You sit in a winged armchair by my head
holding your elbows. I smell you: dirty and sweet.

I think of the way I might have said goodbye.
We tried not to speak of such things.

You turned and your hot face was bright.
I saw myself reflected in it as I left.

2

The room grows cold. I am not arranged in a line.
Lift me, please, from my crookedness.

We need to start again but it is always too late
and I am afraid you do not know how to begin.

3

Love, you surprise me: turning, dipping a cloth
in a shallow bowl, you wipe my palms in slow circles

and twist my rings so that everything is facing
one way. This is touch without touching,

as it always is. You are so quiet, sounds slip
from the ceiling. I am afraid of you, of your gentleness.

You say, *nothing will remain*, and I hear my bones
in your voice: *At home, the dog will always be searching.*

NOTES

Two Mothers (14)
The poem is inspired by Paula Rego's pastel and charcoal drawing on paper entitled 'Girl With Two Mothers' (2000).

I Have My Heart on My Fist (25)
This is Peter Miller's translation of Anne Hébert's poem 'Le Tombeau Des Rois' (1953). The original reads: *'J'ai mon coeur au poing / Comme un faucon aveugle.'*

The Instant of my Death (27)
'The Instant of My Death' is the title of a short story by Maurice Blanchot. It was originally published as 'L'Instant de Ma Mort' (1994).

Operation Dark Harvest (48)
This poem is a response to Carolyn Forché's 'On Earth' (2003). The biblical quotations are from Exodus 9.3 and 9.10.

The Most Quiet (54)
'The most quiet' is a phrase taken from John Taggart's 'Slow Song for Mark Rothko' (1981).

I Have Not Yet Discovered (56)
This is John Felstiner's translation of Paul Celan's 'Tenebrae' (1959). The original reads: *'Es war Blut, es war, / was du vergossen, Herr. // Es gläntze.'*

Cinder (59)
This poem draws on material from Jacques Derrida's *Feu la cendre* (1987) and Ned Luckacher's introduction, 'Mourning Becomes Telepathy' (1991).

Kola Superdeep (61)
The quotation is from Franz Kafka's 'A partial narrative' in *Wedding Preparations in the Country and Other Posthumous Prose Writings* (1953), translated by Ernst Kaiser and Eithne Wilkins. The poem also responds to and echoes a passage from 'The Eight Octavo Note-Books'. Both of these fragments by Kafka are cited by Hélène Cixous in *Three Steps on the Ladder of Writing* (1993), translated by Sarah Cornell and Susan Sellers.

Remains (62)
This quotation is taken from Jacques Derrida's last interview before his death in 2004. The interview was with Jean Birnbaum and appeared in *Le Monde* on 19 August 2004. Derrida died on 8 October 2004.